I Wonder Why

Tunnels Are Round

and Other Questions About Building

Steve Parker

Kingfisher

KINGFISHER
An imprint of Larousse plc
Elsley House, 24-30 Great Titchfield Street,
London, W1P 7AD

First published by Kingfisher 1995
(hb) 10 9 8 7 6 5 4 3 2 1
(pb) 10 9 8 7 6 5 4 3 2 1
Copyright © Larousse plc 1995

A CIP catalogue record for this book is available from the
British Library

ISBN 1 85697 310 7 (hb)
     1 85697 314 X (pb)

Phototypeset by Tradespools Ltd, Frome, Somerset
Printed and bound in Italy

Series editor: Jackie Gaff
Series designer: David West Children's Books
Author: Steve Parker
Art editor: Christina Fraser
Cover illustrations: Chris Forsey, cartoons by Tony Kenyon
   (B.L. Kearley)
Illustrations: Peter Dennis (Linda Rogers Associates) pp. 28-
   29, 30-31; Micheal Fisher (Garden Studio) pp. 18-19,
   24-25; Chris Forsey pp. 4-5, 6-7, 14-15, 20-21 22-23,
   26-27; Tony Kenyon (B.L. Kearley) all cartoons; Roger
   Stewart (Virgil Pomfret Agency) pp. 12-13, 16-17;
   Richard Ward pp. 1, 8-9, 10-11.

CONTENTS

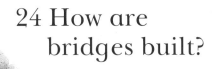

What are houses made from?

Most houses are made from bricks, but they can be built out of almost anything – as long as it's strong and it keeps out the weather. Builders like to use materials they can get hold of easily – bricks or stone, wood, reeds, or mud.

● Bricklayers put mortar between the bricks. Mortar is a mixture of water, sand and cement, and it glues the bricks together.

● Houses protect us from the heat in summer, and the cold and rain in winter.

● There are about 12,000 bricks in the outside walls of a two-storey house.

● Some birds use mud to build their homes, but it's not shaped into little bricks!

● There aren't any bricks in the middle of a forest, but there's plenty of wood for building cabins.

● In the marshes of southern Iraq, in the Middle East, people use bundles of river reeds to build beautiful homes.

● In hot places such as Africa, people often build with mud and straw. The mixture dries hard in the sunshine.

What holds up the ceiling?

The weight of ceilings and floors is carried by strong wooden beams called joists. There are joists hidden away under the floorboards and above the ceiling of every room.

● The roof is held up by thick wooden rafters. Tiles keep out the rain.

Rafter

Joist

● Sometimes uninvited visitors live under the floor, such as the wood-eating grubs of the woodworm beetle.

What's behind the walls?

Among other things, there's usually a lot of air! That's because most brick houses have double outer walls, with a gap between the walls. Pipes and electrical wiring are tucked away in this gap.

● Building a house is teamwork. A plumber lays all the pipes, an electrician does the wiring, and a carpenter puts in the windows, doors and cupboards.

What's under the floor?

There are pipes under the floor. Some carry clean water around the house. Others take dirty water away. Some aren't for water at all – they carry gas, which is burned to heat ovens for cooking and water for washing.

What do bulldozers do?

Bulldozers clear building sites and make the land flat enough to build on. The huge steel blade at the front shifts great mounds of soil, bricks or anything else that's in the way. Bulldozers are incredibly powerful machines – just the job for pushing and shoving things around.

● At the back of some bulldozers there's an arm with large metal spikes called rippers. These are used to break up hard rock and to tear out tree stumps.

● Guess what a small bulldozer is called – a calfdozer!

8

- There are even special under-water bulldozers which flatten riverbeds or the seafloor so that bridges can be built on them.

- A bulldozer once won a tug-of-war contest against 150 people!

Why don't bull-dozers get stuck?

Instead of a tyre on each wheel, a bulldozer has a crawler track around each pair of front and back wheels. Crawler tracks grip the ground well and stop the bulldozer from getting bogged down in the mud.

- Bulldozers can be as much as 500 times heavier than you. But their tracks spread the weight so evenly that they are much less likely to sink in the mud!

Why do houses need holes?

Most houses start with holes in the ground. The holes are filled with runny concrete, which hardens as it sets. The rest of the house is then built on top of this firm base, called the foundations.

● Many diggers have a wide front bucket, as well as the digging bucket at the back.

● A digger can dig a trench as fast as 20 people with spades.

● The biggest earth-scooping buckets can hold five large family cars. They are on huge mining machines called excavators, which are about ten times bigger than the average digger.

● Diggers also dig holes for swimming pools, rubbish heaps and top-secret underground hiding places!

What do diggers do?

A digger does much more than dig. Its wide front bucket is brilliant at scooping rubble into a truck. A scissor-like bucket can also be fitted to the front, to grab and lift logs and pipes.

● A huge hammer can be fitted to a digger, allowing it to smash up rocks.

Do buildings have roots?

Skyscraper foundations are called piles and they are made of steel or concrete. Piles do the same job for a skyscraper as roots do for a tree. They stop it blowing over in the wind, or sinking into the ground under its own weight.

Which are the world's biggest hammers?

To knock a nail into wood, you use a hammer. To drive a steel pile into the ground, builders use a huge hammer called a piledriver. A crane lifts up the piledriver, then drops it on to the pile with a deafening BANG!

Which are the world's largest corkscrews?

Sometimes, the holes for piles are drilled with an auger – a long tool which works like a giant corkscrew, twisting its way deep down into the ground. A steel rod is put into the hole, and then lots of concrete is poured down around it.

● The piles for some skyscrapers are well over 50 metres deep. That's the same as five houses buried one on top of one another!

● Using piledrivers at night is against the law in many towns and cities. They're much too noisy.

Do buildings have a skeleton?

Nowadays, most big buildings have a strong steel framework inside them. This framework does a similar job to the bony skeleton inside your body. It props up the building and stops it from collapsing to the ground.

• Some beams are joined by big nails called rivets. These are punched through holes. Then their ends are flattened to stop them slipping out again.

• Other beams are joined by welding. The ends are heated until they melt and flow together like runny chocolate. When they cool down, the joined ends have hardened together.

• A skyscraper's framework is made from steel beams and tubes. The ends of one kind of beam look like the letters I or H. Beams this shape are stronger and lighter than square beams.

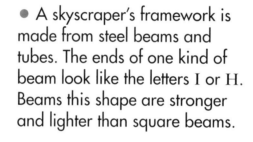

Do buildings have a skin?

The skin of a building is formed by its windows and walls. On modern skyscrapers these are made of glass or plastic panels, and thin concrete or stone sheets. These panels and sheets are called cladding.

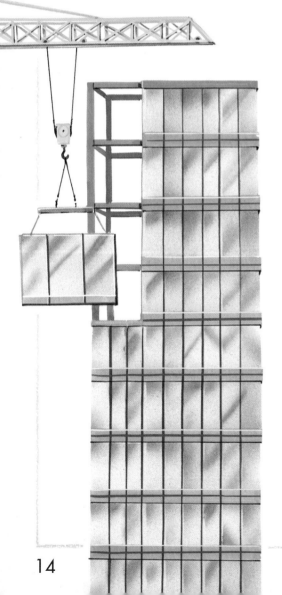

Which are the tallest cranes?

Tower cranes can reach higher than 15 houses piled on top of one another. When builders are putting up a skyscraper, they need a crane this tall to lift the beams and cladding into place.

● The arm of a tower crane is called a jib. As the crane lifts a load at one end of the jib, it's balanced by weights at the other end, rather like balancing a seesaw.

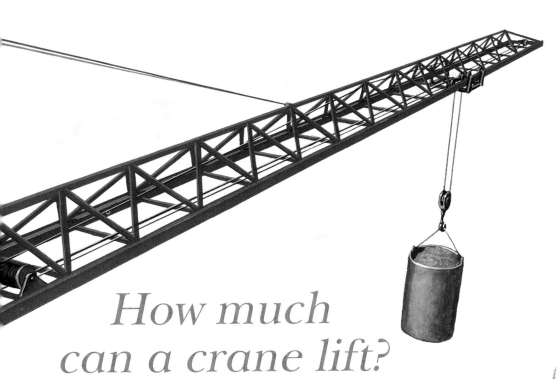

● It's easy to see how building cranes got their name – they're tall and thin, just like the long-legged birds we call cranes.

How much can a crane lift?

The most powerful cranes work at sea on special boats called salvage barges. These cranes can raise a ship weighing more than 5,000 tonnes from the seabed. That's like lifting all the people you could fit into a really massive sports stadium!

● It's a long climb up to the cab of a tower crane. Some cabs have a toilet in them, to save the driver going up and down too often. Phew!

● If you like the idea of driving a crane, be grateful you weren't alive 2,000 years ago. Roman crane drivers were slaves, who were forced to run all day long inside a large wheel called a treadmill.

Which are the world's tallest buildings?

Skyscrapers are the world's tallest buildings – but they've only held the record for 100 years or so. Before then, the world's tallest buildings were the great cathedrals of Europe.

3 The Eiffel Tower, Paris, France, 300 m high, built in 1887-89.

● In some skyscrapers, people live high above the clouds. They have to phone down to find out if it's raining at street level!

1 The Great Pyramid was built 4,500 years ago at Giza, in Egypt. It's 146 m high.

2 Before its spire fell down in 1548, England's Lincoln Cathedral topped 160 m.

● The world's tallest house of cards was well over 4 metres high – that's nearly twice as high as your bedroom ceiling.

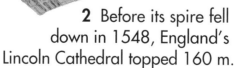

4 The Empire State Building, New York, USA, 381 m high, built in 1929-30.

5 The world's tallest building, the Sears Tower, Chicago, USA, 443 m high, built in 1970-73.

● No one likes climbing stairs, so it's a good thing passenger lifts were invented in the 1850s.

When was the first skyscraper built?

In 1885, the people of Chicago, USA, were amazed to see a ten-storey building being built in their city. It was the world's first skyscraper. Over the next 15 years, the cities of Chicago and New York raced each other to build the world's tallest skyscraper.

Why are some buildings knocked down?

Buildings are knocked down when they are so old or damaged that they're unsafe. Or when someone wants to put a bigger, better building in their place. The quickest way to destroy them is to blow them up with explosives.

● It only takes a few seconds to blow a building up, but it takes a lot longer to work out how to do it safely! Experts decide how much explosive to use, and where to place it.

How do you wreck a building?

You smash it to pieces by swinging a huge metal wrecking ball from a crane! At 10 tonnes, a big wrecking ball weighs as much as 14 cars, and can do a lot of damage as it bashes into a wall.

● A warning whistle or hooter tells everyone that the building is about to explode!

● Canadian karate experts once knocked down a seven-roomed farmhouse with their bare hands and feet in just over 3 hours.

How do you clear up all the mess?

Bulldozers start, by pushing all the rubble into big heaps. Then diggers scoop it up and load it in dump trucks. The trucks drive off to a special rubbish tip and dump their loads. Then they return to the building site for more.

Why are tunnels round?

● The Eurotunnel TBM's cutting head has over 100 cutting rollers and 200 sharp gnashing teeth.

Tunnels are round because drills make round holes! Even tunnels dug with spades have arched roofs. That's because an arch is a much stronger shape than a square. Big tunnels are carved out by tunnel-boring machines (TBMs, for short). These are like gigantic drills, twisting and grinding their way through the ground.

● The Eurotunnel between Britain and France is 50 kilometres long. If all the earth and rock from the tunnel were piled up, it would be as tall as the Eiffel Tower.

How do you tunnel through hard rock?

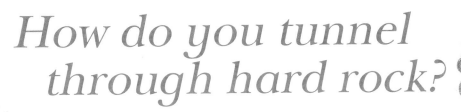

Even the most powerful TBM can't cope with really hard rock. Tunnel-builders have to use explosives to blast their way, a little bit at a time.

● Tunnels aren't just for big things like cars and trains. Smaller tunnels carry electricity cables, as well as gas, water and sewage pipes.

Can a mole dig as fast as a TBM?

A mole can dig five times faster than a TBM, using nothing but its two front paws. It's a lot smaller, though, and so are its tunnels!
You can probably guess what the TBM's nickname is – the mole, of course!

How are bridges built?

Like buildings, bridges start with deep foundation holes. These are filled with metal and concrete, then towers called piers are built on top. The deck is often made from sections, hoisted into place by cranes. Finally, the road or railway is laid on top of the deck.

● Deck sections are brought to the site on barges, towed by tugboats.

● It takes a team of 29 painters three years to paint Scotland's 521-metre-long Forth Railway Bridge. When they finish, they have to start all over again!

Deck

Pier

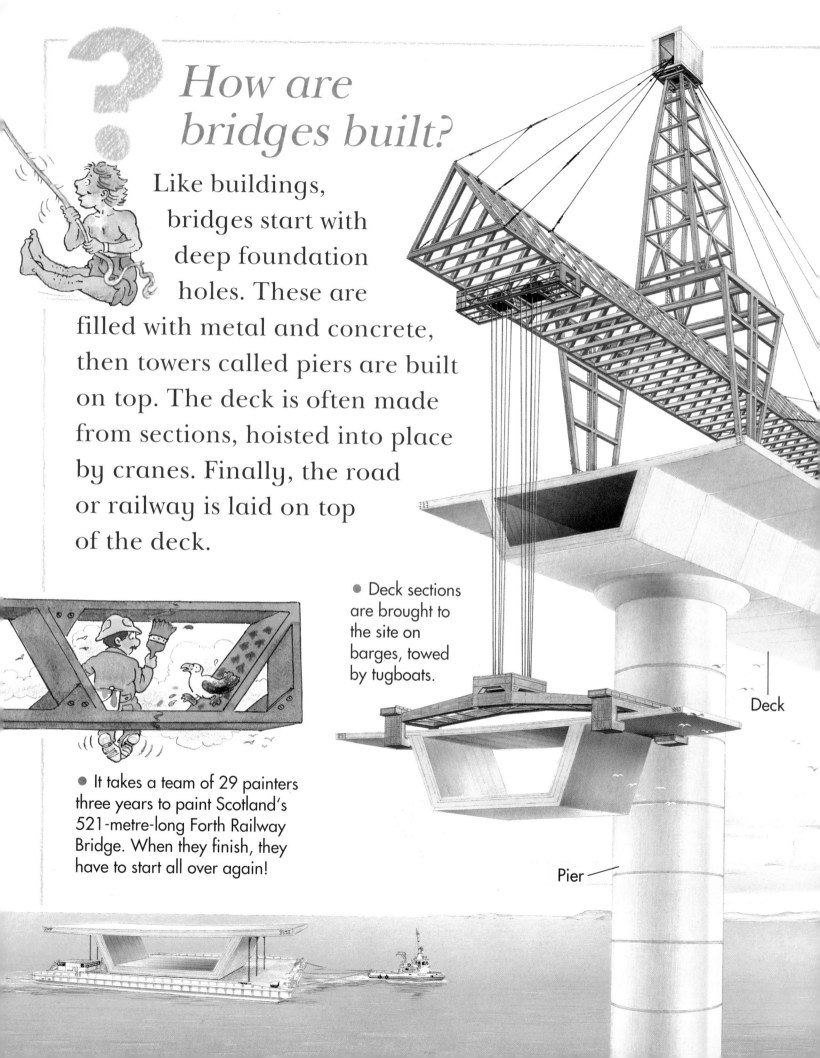

• Soldiers break step when crossing small bridges. If they all marched across in step together, the bridge might bounce. Too much bouncing, and it might break!

• If army ants have to cross gaps, some of them make a living bridge for the others to crawl over.

Do bridges sway about in the wind?

Bridges can bend and sway about as much as 2 or 3 metres – but don't worry, they're meant to! If bridges were completely stiff and rigid, a very strong wind might crack them.

Which bridge can break in two?

London's Tower Bridge carries traffic over the river Thames. The roadway is built in two halves, which can be raised or lowered like drawbridges. When a tall ship sails up the river, each half of the bridge lifts up so that the ship can pass through.

● Bungee-jumpers love the Royal Gorge Bridge in Colorado, USA. At 321 metres above the surface of the river, it's the highest bridge in the world.

● Tower Bridge isn't named for its tall towers, but after its neighbour, the Tower of London.

• The Sydney Harbour Bridge is sometimes nicknamed the coathanger – you can probably see why!

• On some bridges, the whole deck lifts straight up to allow tall ships to sail beneath.

Which is the widest bridge in the world?

At 49 metres, the world's widest bridge is the Sydney Harbour Bridge, in Australia. Two trains, eight cars, a cyclist, and a person walking a dog can all travel side by side across it!

Which bridge can you shop on?

The Ponte Vecchio is lined with shops full of glittering jewellery. The bridge was built over 600 years ago, across the river Arno, in the Italian city of Florence.

Which roof opens when the Sun shines?

The SkyDome sports stadium in Toronto, Canada, has a roof which can open and close. Three gigantic steel panels slide back in good weather to make the stadium open-air. If it starts to rain, the roof closes again – but it takes 20 minutes, so don't forget your umbrella!

● Seafood is so popular in Japan that there's even a fish-shaped restaurant. It's in a large seaport called Kobe.

Which building is inside out?

The outside of the Pompidou Centre in Paris is covered in things that are normally hidden away inside. There are lifts, stairs, water pipes, electricity cables – even toilets. It's rather like having your lungs, muscles and veins on the outside of your body!

● One of the buildings at Disney World in Florida, USA, looks like a giant golf ball. Its walls are made up of hundreds of metal triangles.

① ② ③

● This is how the SkyDome's roof opens wide.

Could people live in space?

They already have! Some astronauts have lived in space stations spinning around the Earth for as long as a year. There are plans for much bigger stations, where people could live for 10 years, and even for settlements on Mars.

● It would take 8 months to reach Mars in a spacecraft. The crew would have to take everything they needed with them – the food for just one person would make a pile twice as big as a family car.

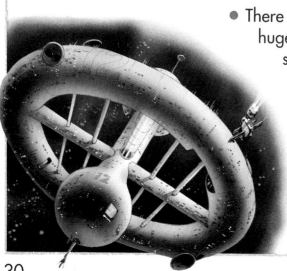

● There are plans for a huge wheel-shaped space station, measuring over 1 kilometre across.

● People have even lived under the sea, but not for longer than a few weeks at a time. They were working in underwater laboratories.

Could people live in a greenhouse?

They already have! In the USA's Arizona Desert there's a gigantic greenhouse called Biosphere II. It's like a miniature Earth, with its own farm, lake and stream, rainforest and desert – there's even a mini-ocean with a coral reef.

● Biosphere II is an experiment. The people who live inside it are completely cut off from the outside world. Scientists are studying whether people could live this way out in space.

Could people live underground?

They already do! In the Australian outback town of Coober Pedy, people dig holes to mine the precious gemstones called opals. They also carve out cool underground homes, to escape from the scorching heat up on the surface.

Index

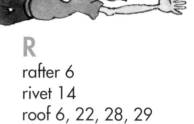